AnimalWays

Cats

AnimalWays

Cats

Rebecca Stefoff

Benchmark Books

MARSHALL CAVENDISH
NEW YORK

For Andy, Harley, Carmen, and Blondie,
with very fond memories.

Benchmark Books
Marshall Cavendish
99 White Plains Road
Tarrytown, NY 10591-9001
www.marshallcavendish.us

Text copyright © 2004 by Rebecca Stefoff
Illustrations copyright © 2004 by Ka Botzis

All Internet sites were available and accurate when sent to press.

Library of Congress Cataloging-in-Publication Data
Stefoff, Rebecca, 1951–
Cats / by Rebecca Stefoff.
p. cm — (Animalways)
Includes bibliographical references (p.) and index.
Contents: Cats and people—How cats developed—The biology of the cat—The life cycle—Feline behavior—Cats today.
ISBN 0-7614-1577-7
1. Cats—Juvenile literature. [1. Cats.] I. Title. II. Series.
SF445.7.S7   2004   636.8—dc21   2002155247

Photo Research by Candlepants Incorporated

Cover Photo: Getty Images/Digital Vision

The photographs in this book are used by permission and through the courtesy of; *AnimalsAnimals:* Scott W. Smith, 2; Robert Maier, 88. *Corbis:* 9; Cynthia Pringle, 10; Scott T. Smith, 12; Historical Picture Archive, 20; Bettmann, 25; Layne Kennedy, 29; Peter Johnson, 32; Jim Zuckerman, 35; Yann Arthur-bertrand, 38, 39, 42, 44, 94; Roger Ressmeyer, 43; Kevin R. Morris, 49; Tim Davis, 51; Jim Zucherman, 61; Joe McDonald, 64; Rick Ergenbright, 67; Paul A. Souders, 68; Roy Morsch, 73; William Gottlieb, 76; Renee Lynn, 85; Al Francekevich, 98; Philip Gould, 102; *Art Resource, NY:* Werner Forman, 15; Erich Lessing, 17; Borromeo, 21; *Peter Arnold:* Martin Harvey, 36. *Image Works:* Syracuse Newspaper/David Lassman, 46. *Getty:* Taxi/Arthur Tilley, 53; Digital Vision, 57 (left); Taxi/Jeffrey Sylvester, 59; Photodisc, 70; The Image Bank/G.K. & Vikki Hart, 75; Digital Vision, 77; Eyewire Collection, 83; Stone/Colin Hawkins, 92; Photo Disc, back cover; *Photo Researchers:* NHPA, 57 (right); Carolyn A. McKeone, 72; Stephen J. Krasemann, 89; Terry Rozo, 100; *Laura Sensabaugh:* lady@ladystardust.com, 80; *Photofest:* 97.

Printed in China

3 5 6 4 2

Contents

Animal Kingdom

CNIDARIANS

coral

ARTHROPODS
(animals with
jointed limbs and
external skeleton)

MOLLUSKS

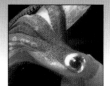

squid

CRUSTACEANS

crab

ARACHNIDS

spider

INSECTS

grasshopper

MYRIAPODS

centipede

CARNIVORES

lion

SEA MAMMALS

whale

PRIMATES

orangutan

HERBIVORES
(5 orders)

elephant

PHYLA

ANNELIDS

earthworm

CHORDATES
(animals with
a dorsal
nerve chord)

ECHINODERMS

starfish

SUB PHYLA

VERTEBRATES
(animals with a
backbone)

CLASSES

FISH

fish

BIRDS

gull

MAMMALS

AMPHIBIANS

frog

REPTILES

snake

ORDERS

RODENTS

squirrel

INSECTIVORES

mole

MARSUPIALS

koala

SMALL MAMMALS
(several orders)

CAT

1 Cats and People

An eighteenth-century English poet named Christopher Smart listed the virtues of the beloved animal he called "my Cat Jeoffry." Smart wrote that "there is nothing sweeter than his peace when at rest" and "there is nothing brisker than his life when in motion." A house without a cat is incomplete, Smart believed—and many people over the past few thousand years have agreed with him. Domestic cats are among the best-loved animals in the world. At the dawn of the twenty-first century, the United States alone had an estimated 75 million pet cats. Familiar as the cat is, however, it has an air of mystery.

Animal-behavior experts and pet owners alike see cats as more independent and self-contained than the other animals that share people's homes and lives. Some say that in spite of domestication, cats are not truly tame. Today's domestic cats belong to the same species as small, hardy felines that still live wild across much of the world, and in the heart of every plump,

From playful kittens to hardworking rat-catchers, no animal is more closely linked to people than the "harmless necessary cat," as William Shakespeare called it.

A PET CAT RUBS SCENT FROM ITS BODY ONTO ITS OWNER'S ANKLES—THE CAT'S WAY
OF SAYING, "THIS PERSON IS MINE." TO THE OWNER, AND MAYBE TO THE CAT AS
WELL, THE RUBBING IS AN ENJOYABLE SHOW OF AFFECTION.

dozing house cat lives a fierce, nimble hunter that prowls and
pounces. Part of the charm of cats to those who love them is
seeing a glimpse of the wild animal in a cat that is chasing string
or playing with a toy—a cat that, moments later, twines affec-
tionately around its owner's ankles or stretches out purring in a

lap. French novelist Victor Hugo claimed that "God made the cat to give humankind the pleasure of caressing the tiger." Few humans have had the privilege of caressing tigers (and lived to tell about it), but almost anyone, anywhere, can stroke a cat. Yet how and why cats came to live with people is not clearly known.

From Wild to Domesticated

The cat is different from all other domestic animals. From elephants to chickens, from camels to pigs, the other creatures that humans have tamed live in groups in the wild. The first animals to be domesticated were wolves, the ancestors of modern dogs. They live in packs. Sheep, goats, cattle, and horses, also domesticated in prehistoric times, live in herds. Guided by inborn instinct and early experiences, all of these animals form communities. Scientists who study animal behavior think that these animals could have been domesticated because they are, in a sense, programmed to live with others and to be guided by a leader or senior member of the pack or herd. Cats, however, lack this kind of programming. Rudyard Kipling, author of *The Jungle Book* and *Just So Stories*, wrote a story called "The Cat That Walked by Himself"—a title that contains an important truth. Cats do walk alone. A few large members of the cat family, such as lions and cheetahs, form groups, but the closest wild relatives of the domestic cat do not.

Domestic cats are members of the species *Felis silvestris*. Nondomestic members of the same species are found in Europe, Asia, and Africa and are known as wildcats (the much larger North American animals known as cougars, pumas, or mountain lions are sometimes wrongly called wildcats, but they belong to an entirely different species, *Felis concolor*). Each wildcat spends its life alone, except in two circumstances. Males and females

CARVED DECORATIONS ON THE CITY AND COUNTY BUILDING IN SALT LAKE CITY, UTAH, INCLUDE THIS CAT CRAWLING OUT OF A FLORAL DESIGN. ALTHOUGH NORTH AMERICA HAS SEVERAL KINDS OF WILD FELINES, THE WILDCAT THAT GAVE RISE TO DOMESTIC CATS IS NOT AMONG THEM.

come together briefly to mate, and kittens spend a few months with their mother and siblings before striking out on their own solitary lives. In its natural state, *Felis silvestris* is clearly not a group animal. But if group living is a requirement for domestication, and wildcats do not come into the world equipped for group living, how did cats become domesticated? The answer may never be fully known, but in recent years researchers have come up with new ideas about how cats' lives became joined with the lives of humans. Those ideas are part of a new and revolutionary view of animal domestication in general.

For centuries, the common view of how domestication had occurred was that prehistoric people, realizing how useful it would be to have captive herds of food animals, began capturing wild animals and breeding them. Over time, by allowing only animals with "tame" characteristics to mate and produce offspring, human beings created animals that were less wild and more dependent upon people. Eventually this process led to the domestic farm animals and pets that we know today, many of which would fare quite badly in the wild, having lost their ancient survival skills and instincts.

Recent research suggests that this view of domestication is incomplete. Prehistoric human beings did capture and breed useful wild animals, and those species became tamer over time (they generally changed physically, too, developing larger bodies and smaller brains than their wild cousins). But specialists in animal behavior now think that domestication was not simply something people did to animals—the animals played an active part in the process. Wolves and wild horses, for example, may have taken the first steps in their own domestication by hanging around human settlements, feeding on people's garbage and crops and getting used to human presence and activity. Individual animals that were not too nervous or fearful to live near people produced offspring that also tolerated humans, making it easier for people to capture and tame them.

In this version, people succeeded in domesticating only animals that had already adapted easily to life around humans. Domestication required an animal that was willing to become domestic. The process was more like a dance with two partners than a triumph of humans over animals.

At first glance, the taming of cats seems to fit nicely into this new story of domestication. A traditional theory says that after prehistoric people in the Near East and Egypt invented agriculture and started farming, rats and mice gathered to feast on their stored grain. Wildcats, in turn, gathered at the same places to prey on the rats and mice. Over time, cats got used to people and people got used to cats, until at some point cats were tame. New studies of wildcats, however, seem to call this theory into question. Wildcats don't share hunting and feeding territories, and they don't live close to people or seek out human settlements as food sources. Experts do not know whether wildcats were partners in their own domestication. They do know that long after people had acquired domestic dogs, sheep, goats, cattle, and horses, they somehow acquired tame cats. By mating the least aggressive cats with one another, they produced animals with increasingly tame qualities. Because the wildcats of Africa are less aggressive and easier to tame than those of Asia or Europe, researchers think that the domestic cat originated in Africa, possibly in ancient Egypt, where the recorded history of the cat begins.

Cats in History

We will never know exactly where or when wildcats were first tamed. It probably happened more than once in the ancient

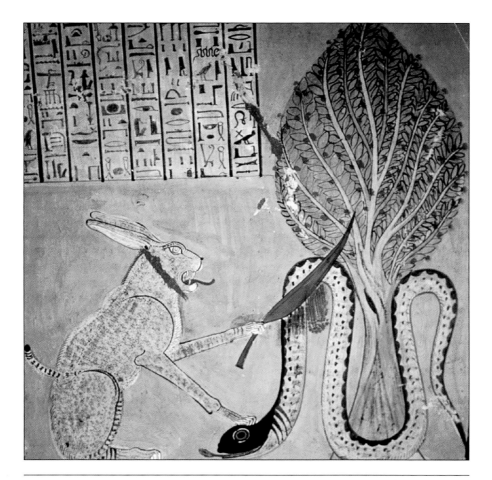

SOME OF THE OLDEST KNOWN IMAGES OF CATS WERE PAINTED OR CARVED IN ANCIENT EGYPT. THIS IMAGE FROM AROUND 1200 B.C. SHOWS THE SUN GOD, RA, IN THE FORM OF A CAT, KILLING THE SNAKE GOD, APOPHIS. IT WAS PAINTED ON THE WALL OF A WORKMAN'S TOMB NEAR THE CITY OF THEBES.

world. Archaeologists found *Felis silvestris* bones dating from about 6700 B.C. in the ruins of the ancient city of Jericho in the Near East, but these could have been the remains of a wild animal. Unlike the Near East, the Mediterranean island of Cyprus has never had a population of wildcats, yet the ruins of a Stone Age settlement there contained a *Felis silvestris* jawbone from about 6000 B.C. The only explanation is that humans carried either the jawbone or the animal to the island. Some researchers believe that the Cyprus jawbone is the oldest known evidence of feline domestication. Others argue that a single bone is not proof of widespread, long-term domestication. Perhaps someone managed to make a pet—or a meal—out of just one animal.

The oldest definite evidence of domestic cats comes from Egypt. Beginning in about 2000 B.C., cats appear in wall paintings in tombs and other ancient Egyptian structures. These images show that cats had become part of daily life. A kitten plays in a man's lap, a cat devours a fish beneath a woman's chair, another cat moves toward a bowl of food left for it. Cats are shown wearing leashes and even earrings. Some cats appear to be helping people hunt birds in marshes. Archaeologists know that the people of ancient Egypt were fascinated by animals and tried to tame many wild creatures, including antelopes and hyenas. They had better luck domesticating the sleek, attractive wildcats they so clearly admired.

To the ancient Egyptians, cats were more than treasured pets and useful rodent exterminators. They also had religious significance. The cat was a symbol of the goddess Bastet or Bast, who appears in paintings and statues as a woman with a cat's head. Bastet was a goddess of fertility, the ability to produce new life. Many wives who wished to become pregnant worshipped Bastet. These women often wore necklaces bearing small charms in the shape of cats. The Egyptians also created cat sculptures in gold, ivory, wood, and stone. Some of these have been found buried along with the Egyptian dead. Archaeologists suggest that ancient Egyptians believed the statues would provide the dead with feline companionship in the afterlife.

Cats grew to be so loved and respected in ancient Egypt that, as a visiting Greek historian wrote, "Whoever kills a cat in Egypt is condemned to death, whether he committed the

CATS WERE WIDELY WORSHIPPED DURING THE FINAL CENTURIES OF ANCIENT
EGYPTIAN CIVILIZATION. THESE STATUES OF BASTET, THE GODDESS OF FERTILITY, DATE
FROM BETWEEN 713 AND 332 B.C. THE SMALL ONES MAY HAVE BEEN WORN AS
CHARMS BY WOMEN WHO HOPED TO BECOME PREGNANT.

crime deliberately or not. The people gather and kill him."
When a household cat died, the entire family showed the tradi-
tional signs of mourning, such as shaving their eyebrows.
Legend says that an enemy used ancient Egypt's fondness for

cats as a military strategy. In 525 B.C. invaders from Persia (now Iran) wanted to capture a fort on the Egyptian frontier. The Persians collected a mass of cats and either carried them into battle or released them just before they attacked. Fearful of harming the cats, the Egyptians refused to fight back, surrendering the fort.

The Egyptians' love of cats reached its height after about 900 B.C. They seem to have thought that all cats belonged in Egypt, for they passed laws forbidding anyone to take a cat out of the country. Some smuggling of cats did occur, and traveling Egyptians who encountered domesticated cats in other countries brought them back to Egypt. In spite of these efforts, the domestic cat gradually spread beyond the borders of Egypt and throughout the Near East. Cats also emerged farther east, in India and China, although it is not clear whether they were descended from Egyptian cats—the peoples of southern and eastern Asia may have domesticated their own wildcats.

The cats of ancient Egypt, however, definitely spread around the Mediterranean Sea. Cats first appeared in the art of ancient Greece around 500 B.C. Romans of the first century B.C. developed a fascination with everything Egyptian, including cats, which became highly fashionable in Rome. By this time Europeans were well aware of cats' usefulness as rodent-catchers. In addition to pet cats and house cats, Mediterranean communities had populations of free-roaming domestic cats that preyed on mice and rats on farms, in warehouses and storehouses, and on ships.

The Romans conquered much of Europe and carried domestic cats throughout their empire. Evidence of cats in the Roman colony in Britain appears in the form of cats' pawprints on clay tiles from the fourth century A.D. In Great Britain and elsewhere, domestic cats probably interbred with the wildcats that are native to northern Europe. As time passed, domestic cats, once associated with the Romans and the rich, became more common on farms and in villages throughout Europe. By the Middle Ages people saw cats as working animals rather than pampered pets. The job of a cat was to kill mice and rats, as shown by a set of laws made in A.D. 936 by a British ruler. He set the value of a newborn kitten at one penny and that of a cat old enough to hunt at four pennies. If someone stole or killed a cat, the cat's owner had to be repaid with grain in an amount determined by the size of the lost animal.

The cat's value as a working animal was also appreciated in medieval Asia. Chinese cats killed the mice that could destroy silkworm cocoons and threaten China's silk industry. In nearby Japan, however, cats became so prized as pets that few remained outdoors to control the rodent population. Desperate farmers tried to frighten mice and rats with painted lanterns and statues in the shape of cats, but these artistic efforts failed. Finally the emperor made it illegal for people to buy or sell cats or to keep them on leashes. This let cats roam freely and resume their rat-catching duties.

The fate of European cats between the thirteenth and seventeenth centuries is a chapter of feline history still under debate. For years historians routinely wrote that cats, especially black cats, were killed by the hundreds of thousands during these centuries because they were thought to be linked to magic, witches, and the devil. A few writers have even argued that church authorities, fearing that cat worship survived as a lingering remnant of some ancient, pre-Christian religion, wanted to wipe out cats altogether. Recent studies of historical documents, however, have yielded a more balanced view of such claims. On a number of occasions popes and other high-ranking churchmen spoke out against cats as evil, and sometimes they singled out black cats. As a result, from time to time communities did hunt

GUEST FOR TEA IS THE TITLE OF THIS JAPANESE ILLUSTRATION. CATS HAVE LONG HAD AN HONORED PLACE IN JAPANESE ART AND FOLKLORE—ALTHOUGH IT IS UNLIKELY THAT MANY OF THEM HAVE ACTUALLY RECEIVED INVITATIONS TO TEA PARTIES.

down and slaughter large numbers of cats—in some French towns, for example, gangs of citizens hunted down black cats and threw them into bonfires on certain religious holidays. No doubt a great many other cats met undeserved deaths as well.

Cats, however, were not the only animals to suffer at the hands of superstitious and cruel people. Europeans also attacked goats, pigs, dogs, and other animals that they imagined to be associated with witches. There is no evidence of an organized or

A COMIC DRAWING OF A GROUP OF MICE MEETING A CAT, PAINTED ON THE WALL OF A CHRISTIAN MONASTERY IN THE SIXTH CENTURY A.D. MANY CARTOONS AND STORIES HAVE USED CATS AND MICE AS SYMBOLS OF TWO GROUPS IN CONFLICT, OR OF THE STRUGGLE BETWEEN THE POWERFUL AND THE MEEK.

widespread movement to exterminate cats, and there is plenty of evidence that many people, including at least one pope and numerous other churchmen, continued to admire cats, to use them as rat-catchers, and to treasure them as pets. The truth seems to be that while being a cat in Europe in the late Middle Ages or the early modern era was no picnic, neither was it an automatic death sentence.

Cats were especially useful on ships, where the destruction

of precious food supplies by rats was always a problem. Seafaring Europeans carried domestic cats around the world, introducing them to places that had no native wildcats. Among the goods that the Pilgrims brought to their North American colony were several cats that proved their worth by keeping mice out of the colonists' dwindling store of grain. Several centuries later, when Americans were settling their western frontier, cats were so sought after in the new towns of the West that in 1876 a clever trader hauled a wagonload of cats to Deadwood, South Dakota, and sold them by the pound to local shopkeepers and ranchers. Yet the arrival of cats in new environments was not always a good thing. When cats reached places with no native wildcat populations, such as the islands of Hawaii and New Zealand, they destroyed entire species of birds and small animals that had no experience avoiding such successful predators.

Cats in Legend and Lore

Since the dawn of history, cats have stalked soft-footed through the human imagination. They appear in the art, myth, folklore, and literature of many cultures. Some stories and sayings portray cats in a positive way, as wondrous bringers of good fortune. Others paint cats in dark colors, as omens of disaster. The cat's dual image in legend and lore reflects the mixed feelings people have had toward these appealing yet aloof creatures over the ages.

"I am born of the divine She-cat. . . . I am born of the sacred She-cat," declares the god Osiris in the ancient Egyptian text known as the Book of the Dead. Many ancient cultures associated cats with birth and fertility, perhaps because female cats occasionally bear twelve or more young. At the sites of ancient Roman colonies in France, archaeologists have found stone statues of half-naked young men cradling cats in their arms, fertility symbols that the Romans believed would help their families last for many generations.

The association of cats with fertility may lie behind old customs that link cats to the rain that is needed to make cropland fertile. In the southeastern Asian country of Cambodia, for example, farmers traditionally carried a cat from village to village, sprinkling it with water, to encourage the gods to send rain. Grimmer customs in some countries involved sacrificing cats when new fields were plowed or new buildings were constructed. Still other superstitions said that killing a cat brought bad luck because cats were protected by demons, spirits, or magical powers.

People often viewed cats as creatures of darkness, probably because cats hunt and are active at night and because they can see better in dark conditions than humans can. Cats became associated with the night, the moon, and pagan or pre-Christian moon goddesses such as Selene of Greece and Diana of Rome. Cats' supposed connection with paganism, devils, and darkness gave rise to folklore that presents cats as mysterious, frightening, threatening, or treacherous. Superstitious people in many parts of Europe (and later America) believed that cats killed babies in their cradles by sucking their breath. A cat on or near a grave meant that the devil owned the dead person's soul. In some parts of Italy, people feared that if they spoke of someone newly dead, he or she would return with a cat's face. The French and Belgians believed that cats spread their secrets—cats that willingly came to be petted were most likely to betray their owners in this way. Folktales from many European countries link cats to witches. Many stories tell of a cat that attacks a man, usually a traveler at night in a lonely place. He manages to injure the cat and escapes. The next morning a woman in a nearby village is found to have an injury just like that given to the cat—proof that the woman is a witch who can take feline form.

Cats have been linked to both bad luck and good. According to some old superstitions, cats were so unlucky that even a glimpse or a dream of a cat was a sign of coming misfortune. Seeing a cat on the first day of the year meant bad luck for the entire year. In Asia, where white is the color associated with death and funerals, white cats were considered unlucky. Some Europeans and Americans considered white cats lucky but dreaded the bad luck brought by black cats. Edgar Allan Poe, the American master of horror and suspense writing, put a new twist on this tradition in "The Black Cat," a story in which a crazed, drunken murderer's crime is revealed by a black cat he has tormented. Yet Poe, who adored his own feline pet, made the innocent black cat of the story a symbol of justice and the killer's conscience as well as of doom.

In some folktales and superstitions, cats bring good fortune. The English used to say that a man who was kind to cats would find a pretty wife. The French told stories of a cat called the *matagot*. Those who mistreated the *matagot* would come to a bad end, but those who were kind to it reaped unexpected rewards. The French fairy tale "Puss in Boots" is a *matagot* story: A poor young man spares the life of his only possession, a cat, that then uses its wits to gain a kingdom and a bride for its master. The

matagot also appears in the legend of Dick Whittington, a poor boy who became mayor of London with the help of his clever cat.

Japanese folklore also connects cats with good fortune. Japan is the home of a distinctive, short-tailed type of cat called the Japanese bobtail. Traditionally, sailors believed that bobtails with coats of mixed white, black, and tan offered protection against storms and bad weather. One particular lucky cat owes its origin to an old legend about a group of warriors who saw a cat sitting outside a temple holding up one paw. Thinking that the cat was motioning for them to enter, the warriors went into the temple and had tea with the monk. A violent storm broke outside. The warriors realized that the cat's gesture had saved them from being caught in the storm, and their master built a shrine to honor the animal. Over time the *maneki neko*, a mostly white cat beckoning or greeting with one upraised paw, became a symbol of welcome and prosperity. Statues and other images of this kitty still appear throughout Japan and, as a result of international marketing, around the world.

Writers and artists over the centuries have celebrated their cats in words and pictures. A monk in eighth-century Ireland wrote a poem about his cat, and while the monk's name is lost to history, we know that the cat was called Pangur Bán. Twelve centuries later, American journalist Cleveland Amory wrote three books about Polar Bear, a cat he found in the snow. Playwright Karel Čapek of Czechoslovakia surrounded himself with dozens of cats and joked that they were numerous enough to "rule the universe." During the Italian Renaissance, the great artist Leonardo da Vinci often sketched or painted cats, saying that "even the smallest feline is a work of art." Nineteenth-century artist and writer Edward Lear drew many amusing pictures of his cat Foss—a pet so prized that when Lear built a new house he had it made just like his old one so that the elderly Foss would not be confused. More recently, twentieth-century Japanese artist Tsogouhara Foujita painted several portraits of himself, brush in hand, with one of his cats looking over his shoulder. These images capture the enduring bond of curiosity and affection between people and the free-spirited felines that have agreed to share their lives.

2 How Cats Developed

Domestic cats have been with us only a few thousand years, but other cats have been around for much longer than that. Today's cat is the result of millions of years of evolution which prepared it for an existence very different from that of most felines. Yet evolution has also shown that cats are extremely good at adapting to new circumstances and environments. In fact, millions of cats have adapted to living in the caves of large, noisy primates, even going so far as to sleep on these creatures' beds and easy chairs.

Feline Origins

Cats are carnivores, or eaters of meat. Like all carnivorous mammals in the world today, from walruses to weasels, they are descended from a group of small mammals that appeared after the dinosaurs became extinct some 65 million years ago. Scientists

IN THE HANDS OF A SKILLED PALEONTOLOGIST AT SOUTH DAKOTA'S BLACK HILLS INSTITUTE OF GEOLOGICAL RESEARCH, THE FOSSILIZED SKULL OF A LARGE, ANCIENT FELINE SLOWLY EMERGES FROM THE SURROUNDING ROCK.

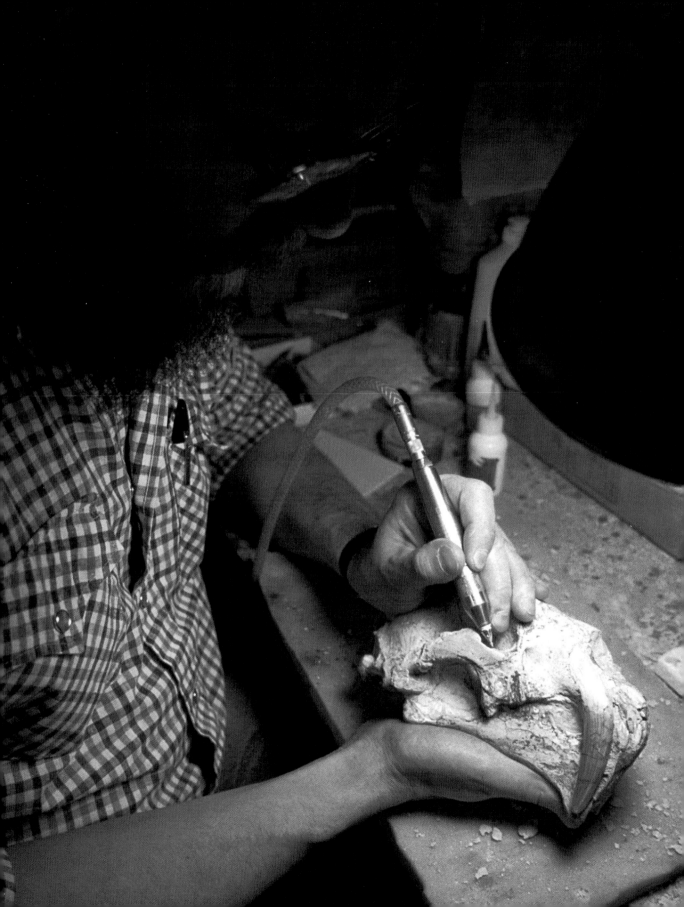

call these little mammals the miacids. The miacids were the first animals to have carnassial teeth, which are large, flesh-tearing teeth found in the jaws of all modern meat-eating mammals.

Over the next 10 million years or so, the miacids evolved into several different groups of carnivores. Scientists call one of these groups aeluroids, from the Latin word for "catlike." The aeluroids were the ancestors of all modern cats, large and small. Over long ages, various species of aeluroids died out, while new species emerged. By about 40 million years ago, the aeluroids had evolved into several families. One of these families was the Felidae, or cats. All of the cat species that exist today are felids, which means that they belong to this family. Many other Felidae species are now extinct.

Around 20 million years ago, some felids began to have many of the characteristics of modern cats. By about 12 million years ago the felids had divided into several subfamilies. Four of these subfamilies later died out completely. The fifth subfamily included the ancestors of all modern cats, from tigers to tabbies. Scientists call this subfamily the Felinae, or felines. The Felinae subfamily gradually evolved into several lines of descent that led to the various kinds of modern cats. The line that led to the small cats emerged around 3 million years ago. A million years later, another line of descent split off from the small-cat line. It led eventually to the species we know today as *Felis silvestris*, which has existed in its present form for at least a quarter of a million years, and possibly longer.

Felis silvestris fossils have been found in many parts of Europe, Asia, and Africa. The oldest fossils come from northern Europe. Scientists believe that the wildcat evolved there, then migrated into Asia. It came to Africa later—genetic studies of wildcat populations suggest that the African wildcat most likely split off from the European population as recently as 20,000

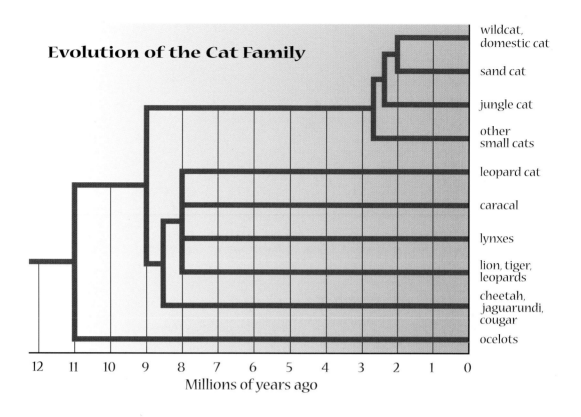

Evolution of the Cat Family

wildcat, domestic cat

sand cat

jungle cat

other small cats

leopard cat

caracal

lynxes

lion, tiger, leopards

cheetah, jaguarundi, cougar

ocelots

| 12 | 11 | 10 | 9 | 8 | 7 | 6 | 5 | 4 | 3 | 2 | 1 | 0 |

Millions of years ago

years ago. But wildcats never existed in the Americas, Antarctica, Australia, or the Pacific Islands. Only after *Felis silvestris* became domesticated did its range expand to cover the world.

Wildcats and Their Relatives

The name *Felis silvestris* means "cat of the forests" in Latin, but wildcats adapted to live in a wide variety of habitats. As Stephen Budiansky writes in *The Character of Cats*, "Wildcats are found from the jungles of Africa to the northern woodlands of Scotland; they live in the deserts of Saudi Arabia and the Sahara, the semideserts of Central Asia, along seacoasts, in rocky scrublands, deciduous forests, and swamps." Within the

A HUNTER IN BOTSWANA DISPLAYS A WILDCAT—*FELIS SILVESTRIS*, THE SAME SPECIES AS DOMESTIC CATS—THAT HE DUG OUT OF A HOLE. IN SOME PARTS OF THE WORLD PEOPLE HUNT CATS FOR FOOD OR FOR THEIR SKINS.

wildcat's range, the only habitats that it does not occupy are tropical rainforests, treeless grasslands, and places where snow lies on the ground for more than a hundred days each year.

Seeing wildcats across such a wide range and in such varied habitats, zoologists used to regard them as three different species: *Felis silvestris* in Europe, *Felis ornata* in Asia, and *Felis lybica* in Africa. They regarded domestic cats as a fourth species, separate from wildcats although clearly related to them. Most zoologists used the name *Felis catus* for the domestic cat. Some reference works still list these names, presenting cats as four species. The latest scientific theory of wildcats and domestic cats, though, is that they all belong to one species. Understanding this new theory requires some knowledge of taxonomy, the system of scientific classification of living things.

Scientists divide all living things into groups on the basis of shared characteristics. Taxonomy begins by assigning each organism to one of several very large groups called kingdoms. After kingdoms are a descending series of levels or categories, each more narrowly defined than the one before it. The taxonomic classification of cats begins with the kingdom Animalia and moves through the phylum Chordata (all animals with backbones), the class Mammalia (all mammals), the order Carnivora (all mammals that are carnivores), the family Felidae (all cats), the subfamily Felinae (all thirty-seven kinds of modern cats), and the genus *Felis* (several dozen small modern cats).

The next—most specific—level is the species, and there scientists sometimes disagree because they are still working out exactly how to define a species. In the past, small differences in coloring and behavior among the different kinds of wildcats led experts to call each population a distinct species. Today, however, zoologists can use DNA analysis to find out just how close or far apart these animals are at the genetic level. DNA studies show only tiny differences among the European, Asiatic, and African wildcats. In addition, the three are very similar in anatomy, or internal structure, and they can all interbreed with one another and produce offspring that are fertile, or capable of reproducing. For these reasons the new trend in cat science is to regard all wildcats as members of the same species, *Felis silvestris*. Some zoologists label the different regional populations as subspecies, calling them *Felis silvestris silvestris*, *Felis silvestris ornata*, and *Felis silvestris lybica*. Others simply call them the silvestris, ornata, and lybica groups within the species. (A few also give the wildcats of Scotland their own subspecies or group name, grampia.)

What about domestic cats? In terms of DNA, anatomy, and ability to interbreed, they are as close to wildcats as wildcats are to one another. Most cat researchers no longer regard domestic cats as a separate species. They do, however, consider them to be a subspecies, *Felis silvestris catus*.

The closest relatives of *Felis silvestris* are other members of the genus *Felis*, especially small cats that resemble the wildcat in size and way of life. Among these are the sand cat of North Africa and the Near East, the leopard cat of southern Asia, and the jungle cat of Egypt and southern Asia. Several of these species can interbreed with *Felis silvestris*, although they do not normally do so in the wild. More distantly related are the large cats: lions, tigers, leopards, jaguars, and cheetahs.

THE SAND CAT LIVES IN NORTH AFRICA AND THE NEAR EAST. TRUE TO ITS NAME, IT CAN SURVIVE IN DRY AREAS—IT LIVES ON THE FRINGES OF DESERTS, PREYING ON LIZARDS, RODENTS, AND INSECTS. SAND CATS ARE SIMILAR IN SIZE AND APPEARANCE TO WILDCATS.

Large felines, such as these African cheetahs, are related to *Felis silvestris*, but that does not stop them from regarding wildcats and other small feline species as prey.

Modern Cat Breeds

What does it mean to say that a cat belongs to a particular breed? A breed is a type of animal with visible differences from others of its species. Some breeds of domestic cats have easily recognizable characteristics. Siamese cats, for example, have blue eyes and distinctive coloring, with cream bodies and a darker shade on the head, paws, and tail (cat breeders call these body parts points when they have special coloring). Persian cats have long, thick fur and flat, shortened faces. Cornish Rex cats have curly, very short hair. Manx cats have no tails. How did these differences arise?

All wildcats have pretty much the same coloring: a grayish background with darker stripes on the body, legs, and tail. Cat scientists call this coloring "mackerel tabby." Mackerel (for a striped fish) describes the black stripes on gray. Tabby is a type of mottled, speckled, or striped overall patterning that appears when each hair is banded with alternating strips of light and dark colors, ending with dark tips. Also known as agouti, tabby coloration probably evolved in wildcats to offer them some camouflage, breaking up the outline of the cat's body and helping it blend into shadows or brush. Although tabby coloration occurs in animals other than cats, the term has become so closely linked to cats that the animals are themselves sometimes called tabbies.

European wildcats tend to have thicker, denser fur than the other groups, especially in winter, and their tabby coloration and mackerel stripes may be more distinct. African wildcats often have red or reddish-brown fur on their ears. Asiatic wildcats can have markings that are closer to spots than stripes. These differences, however, do not occur in every member of each group, and they are very small differences. They are a far

EACH BREED OF DOMESTIC CAT HAS ONE OR MORE DISTINCTIVE FEATURES, SUCH AS THE SHORT, CURLY HAIR OF THE CORNISH REX (LEFT), AND THE VERY SHORT TAIL STUB OF THE "TAILLESS" MANX.

cry from the Persian's squashed-looking face or the Cornish Rex's wiry coat.

Modern breeds arose fairly recently. Once cats became domesticated, people began having favorites and making choices. At first people did not necessarily breed specific pairs of cats to create a certain type of offspring, but they did favor and protect cats with certain features. These cats survived to pass their genes—and their special features—along to future generations.

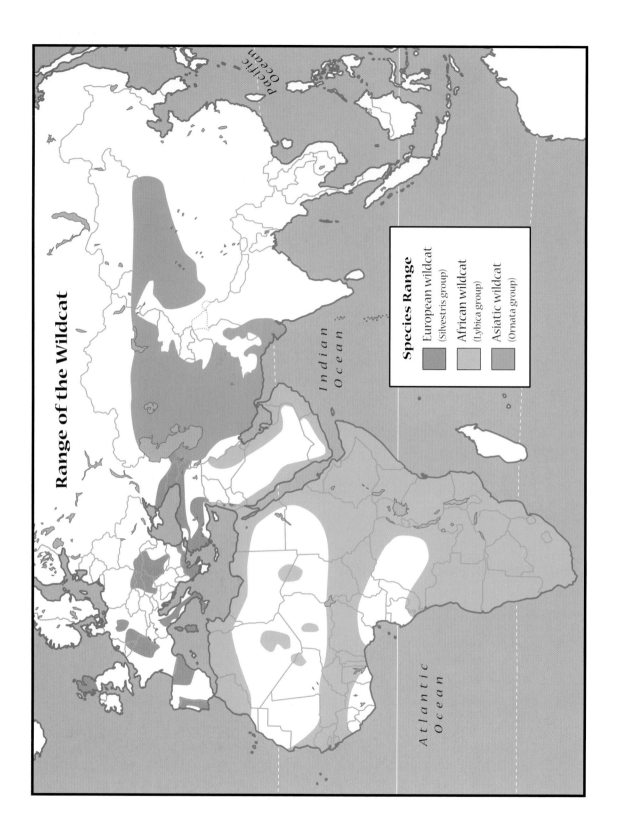

Range of the Wildcat

Pacific Ocean

Indian Ocean

Atlantic Ocean

Species Range

European wildcat
(Silvestris group)

African wildcat
(Lybica group)

Asiatic wildcat
(Ornata group)

Mutations are accidental, natural, and frequently occurring changes to one or more genes. Sometimes their effects are severe, causing an animal's death or making it harder for the animal to survive in the wild. For example, mutations leading to deafness or to all-white coats would create serious disadvantages for wildcats. Sometimes, however, mutations produce changes that either have no effect or increase the animal's chances of surviving and breeding. Useful features such as tabby coloration are the results of favorable mutations. After cats became domesticated, random mutations continued to produce unusual features that had no survival value. Now, however, people admired and valued some of these features and chose those animals as pets or companions.

In addition, cats that lived with people were spared the wildcats' struggle for survival. Having noticeable coloring or long, tangle-prone fur was not a great drawback for a domestic cat. As a result of cats' new conditions, variations began to appear among them—solid-colored cats in white and other colors, spotted cats, and longhaired cats. Some regions developed highly distinctive felines, such as the longhaired Norwegian Forest, Siberian, and Turkish Angora cats, the tailless Manx from Great Britain's Isle of Man, and the blue-black Korat and two-toned Siamese of Thailand.

People then learned to take advantage of naturally occurring variations by deliberately breeding particular cats together to preserve or even strengthen features that they found interesting. In this way they began to develop specific types that they called breeds. By the nineteenth century, Europeans and Americans had started displaying livestock and pets, including cats, in competitive shows. Around this time cat breeding became more ambitious and organized. Cat fanciers—people who breed and raise cats—began developing many new breeds. Persian cats, for example,

THE NORWEGIAN FOREST CAT, KNOWN AS THE *SKAUCATT* OR *SKOGCATT* IN ITS COUNTRY OF ORIGIN, HAS LIVED IN NORWAY FOR HUNDREDS OF YEARS. IT MAY BE DESCENDED FROM MATINGS BETWEEN LOCAL WILDCATS AND LONGHAIRED DOMESTIC CATS BROUGHT FROM TURKEY BY WANDERING VIKINGS.

were created in nineteenth-century Britain by breeders who crossed various longhaired cats from Russia, Turkey, and northern Asia in the hope of creating cats with dense, long coats in certain colors. The Persian's shortened face, the result of a mutation, was an unexpected side effect that became a defining feature of the breed. During the 1920s and 1930s breeders crossed Persians with

THE KORAT IS A SYMBOL OF LUCK IN ITS NATIVE THAILAND, WHERE IT IS CALLED THE *SI-SAWAT*. UNLIKE MOST CATS, KORATS SHED VERY LITTLE FUR. SOME PEOPLE WHO ARE ALLERGIC OR SENSITIVE TO CATS CAN ENJOY THE COMPANY OF KORATS WITHOUT DISCOMFORT.

Siamese cats to create a breed known as the Colorpoint Longhair or Himalayan, which has the Persian's long fur and the Siamese's two-toned coloration and blue eyes.

The process of creating new breeds continues. Some breeds begin with accidental mutations. In 1961, a cat on a Scottish farm gave birth to a kitten whose ears were folded tightly forward. Its descendants, when paired with normal-eared cats, produced more kittens with folded ears—the first of the breed now known as the Scottish Fold. Another new breed, the Selkirk Rex, began with a curly-haired kitten born in Wyoming in 1987. In both cases, an unexpected mutation produced the original cat, and then, controlled breeding produced a population with the same characteristics. Other new varieties have been deliberately created by breeders. During the 1960s, crossbreeding of Abyssinians

NOT ALL KITTENS BORN TO SCOTTISH FOLD CATS HAVE THE TURNED-DOWN EARS THAT ARE THE BREED'S HALLMARK. THE EAR MUTATION IS RARE, MAKING THE SCOTTISH FOLD A SOMEWHAT SCARCE AND SOUGHT-AFTER FELINE.

and Siamese led to a shorthaired, spotted breed called the Ocicat. More recently, controlled crossbreeding between domestic cats and members of an entirely different species—the small, wild leopard cat of Asia—produced the Bengal cat. Similarly, crosses between domestic cats and a small wild feline called Geoffroy's cat produced a breed known as the Safari.

Several organizations around the world regulate cat breeding. One of the first was the Cat Fanciers' Association (CFA), founded in 1906 and now mainly serving North America. The chief British organization is the Governing Council of the Cat Fancy (GCCF), founded in 1910. European cat fanciers established an overall governing body in 1949. One of the newest organizations is the International Cat Association, founded in 1979. Unlike the other groups, which define breeds by physical appearance, the International Cat Association collects genetic information.

Each organization sets standards for the breeds it recognizes. (They don't all recognize the same breeds, and none of them recognizes all of the new varieties created by breeders in recent years.) The CFA, for example, recognizes thirty-seven breeds for championship competition and three others in its "miscellaneous" category. These organizations also run cat shows, spread information about cat breeding and cat care, and maintain registries, or lists, of the cats belonging to each breed. These registries are the source of pedigrees, documents proving that a purebred cat comes from ancestors that were registered breed members.

Cat breeders and animal scientists sometimes disagree on breed characteristics. Breeds are defined by coat color, hair length, markings, and some features of body shape, such as long or short noses, narrow or round heads, and slim or stocky bodies. Breeders may also claim that cats of a particular breed have certain personality or behavior qualities. A breed may be said to be

According to the Cat Fancier's Association, the most popular breed of cat in the world is the Persian, even though the cat's long fur requires regular grooming by the owner. Before appearing in a cat show, this silver tabby Persian receives a dusting of talcum powder to beautify its fur.

"high-strung," for example, or friendly, shy, possessive, easygoing, restless, or unusually clever. Such claims rest largely on casual stories told by cat owners and are extremely hard to test. Some of them are simply ridiculous, such as the claim that the Ragdoll, a new American breed, is unusually relaxed and immune to pain because it descended from a female cat injured in a car accident—an event that would have no effect at all on the genetic makeup of that cat's offspring!

Research suggests that individual cats vary greatly in personality and behavior, regardless of the breed. Individual differences are probably as great as any differences among breeds. The range of variation is also limited where physical differences are concerned. Cat breeds show much less variety than breeds of dogs and horses, which have been domesticated for much longer than cats and have been bred for specific purposes. From the scientific point of view, the differences between cat breeds are very slight—"little more than skin deep," according to animal researcher Stephen Budiansky. And although the lore of breeds and the beauty of purebred cats fascinate lots of people, pedigreed animals form a very small part of the cat population. Only about 3 percent of the 75 million domestic cats in the United States are pedigreed, and the figure is probably the same or lower for the world as a whole. Most cats are mixed-breed felines of no special parentage—simply graceful, elegant examples of *Felis silvestris*.

3 The Biology of the Cat

House cats today still move with "the old, free, pantherlike tread" and still have "the self-reliant watchfulness" of wild animals, wrote cat-loving British author H. H. Munro, better known as Saki. He was right. The movements and senses of the domestic cat, and other features of its biology, remain almost identical to those of its untamed cousins, the free-roaming wildcats.

Physical Features

Adult male domestic cats typically weigh between 8 and 15 pounds (3.5 and 7 kg), females between 5.5 and 10 pounds (2.5 and 4.5 kg). Some cats are heavier, and pet cats whose owners indulge them with excessive food have been known to become quite fat and to weigh as much as 43 pounds (19.5 kg).

The cat's shape and its ability to move depend upon its skeleton, the body's framework. On average, a cat's skeleton contains

CATS ARE VERY GRACEFUL ANIMALS, THANKS TO THEIR FLEXIBLE SKELETONS, STRONG MUSCLES, AND SHARP EYES. CATS USUALLY MOVE SMOOTHLY, SOFTLY, AND QUIETLY, WHICH IS WHY AMERICAN POET CARL SANDBURG WROTE THAT "THE FOG COMES IN ON LITTLE CAT FEET."

240 bones—the number varies slightly according to the length of the animal's tail. Some of these bones give feline anatomy its distinctive features. The cat's femur, or thighbone, is quite long for the animal's size, which helps the cat run fast and jump high. The spine, or backbone, made up of small bones called vertebrae, is unusually flexible. This accounts for the cat's smooth, fluid motions and its great ability to roll, twist, and stretch. Cats are so flexible that they can curl into U-shapes or twist the front half of their bodies in one direction and the rear half in another. The cat's

Cat Skeleton

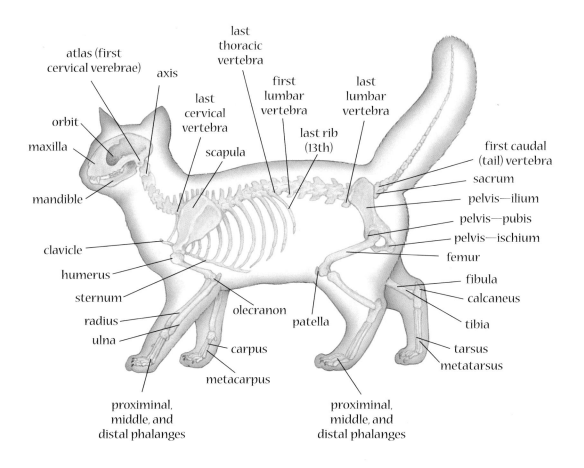

Cat Face

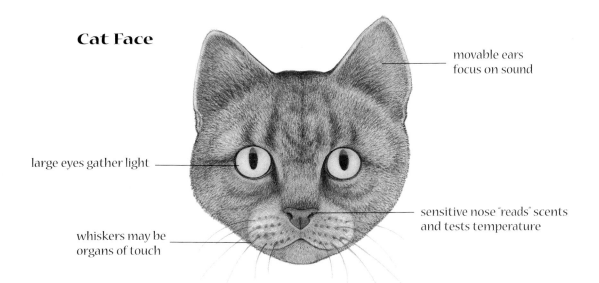

large eyes gather light

movable ears
focus on sound

sensitive nose "reads" scents
and tests temperature

whiskers may be
organs of touch

WHERE THE HEAD CAN GO, THE BODY CAN FOLLOW. CATS ARE ABLE TO SQUEEZE THROUGH TIGHT PLACES BECAUSE THEIR COLLARBONES AND SHOULDER BLADES BEND AND TWIST SLIGHTLY.

clavicle, or collarbone, is very small and not firmly connected to the shoulder. This feature also contributes to feline flexibility. Cats can squeeze through narrow places because their collarbones move easily and can compress together.

Cats walk on their toes. The other bones in their feet do not touch the ground. This type of stride is called digitigrade, in contrast to the plantigrade, or flat-footed, stride of creatures such as people and bears. Digitigrade motion is ideal for predators because it combines speed with stability and allows them to make sharp turns and quick changes of direction. The cat's toes end in bones that are attached to nails or claws made of tough, hard material like horn. One interesting feature of these claws is that, unlike dogs' claws, they can be retracted (drawn back) into a sheath inside the paw. Special muscles attached to the toe bones control the movement of the claws, which cats normally keep retracted unless they need them for climbing, fighting, or scratching. With claws drawn in, the cat's paws and toes are soft, fleshy pads separated and cushioned by tufts of fur.

Cat Paw and Claw

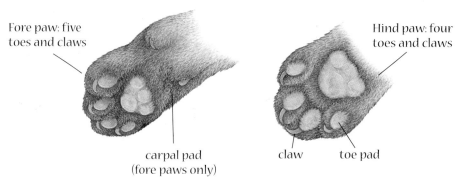

Fore paw: five toes and claws

Hind paw: four toes and claws

carpal pad
(fore paws only)

claw   toe pad

One of the largest bones is the skull, which protects the brain and sense organs. Cats' skulls have several features related to the wildcat's natural way of life. Compared with the skulls of most other mammals, including humans, cats' skulls have eye sockets that are huge in proportion to the size of the skull. The cat's large eyes give it the ability to see well in low or dim light—a useful trait for an animal that often hunts at night. Another key feature of the carnivore's skull is its set of thirty sharp teeth. Four knife-like canine teeth, two each in the upper and lower jaws, stab

THOUGH THE FOUR LONG, SHARP TEETH IN A CAT'S JAW ARE CALLED CANINE TEETH, THEY HAVE NOTHING TO DO WITH DOGS. THEY ARE AMONG THIS FELINE PREDATOR'S MOST IMPORTANT TOOLS. ALSO IMPORTANT ARE THE LARGE EYES. BY GATHERING AS MUCH LIGHT AS POSSIBLE, THEY ALLOW THE ANIMAL TO SEE IN DIM LIGHT OR SEMIDARKNESS.

prey. Behind them are teeth that cut and shear meat into bites small enough to swallow. (Cats do not chew their food but rather gulp it down in chunks.) Between the canine teeth are small, straight front teeth called incisors, perfect for gentle nipping. Cats use them in grooming to pluck fleas, grit, sand, or snarls out of their fur.

Cats have extremely strong muscles in their hindquarters to power many movements. When cats walk or run, the energy for forward motion comes mainly from their hind legs, while their front legs provide balance and act as brakes. Cats can run fast but cannot keep up high speeds for long. Their lungs are small in relation to their overall body size, which means that they quickly run out of oxygen and become tired. This is not a problem for most types of cats because they generally catch their prey by leaping or pouncing on it rather than running it down. Cats are sprinters, not marathon runners.

The strong muscles of a cat's hind legs are like springs that let the animal jump up to five or six times its own height. Many a cat owner has been surprised to find a pet perched atop a refrigerator or a fence thought to be out of reach. The rear legs also provide power for climbing. A climb up a tree or pole usually begins with a short upward leap. Upon landing the cat extends its rear claws and pushes its way up. Whether climbing or jumping, however, cats sometimes find that going up is easier than getting down. A cat faced with a big downward jump slides the front part of its body down as far as possible before it jumps. This eases the shock on the front legs, which are less strong than the hind legs.

Climbing down also presents problems, as the rear-curving claws offer little gripping power when the cat is moving head first down a tree trunk. A cat may therefore climb down a tree backward, although it dislikes being unable to see what is behind

Cat Muscles

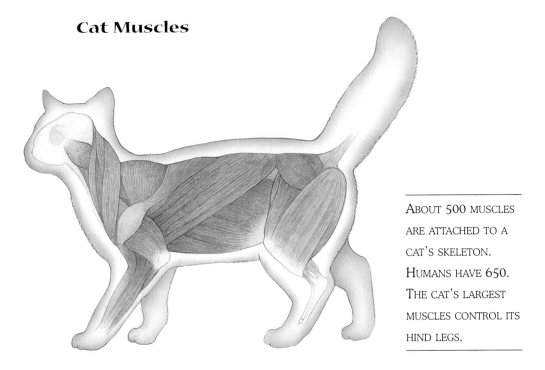

or below it. If the height is not too great, it may climb down head first in a combination of slithering, scrambling, and jumping. Sometimes, however, cats remain high in a tree or on a roof for a long time, until someone rescues them.

The cat's flexible skeleton and excellent muscle tone let it move in ways impossible for humans. When stalking prey, cats can move extremely slowly, smoothly controlling even their slightest motion, or they can freeze in almost any position for a long time. Cats also have excellent balance and can walk easily along narrow fence tops and railings. Movements of the flexible tail help the cat maintain its balance. Perhaps the cat's most famous movement is the one animal scientists call the self-righting reflex—the movement that allows falling cats to land on their feet. The cat seems to right itself in a fraction of a second, but scientists have figured out how it is done by dropping cats (from modest heights and onto padded surfaces, of course!), photographing the falls, and studying the results. They learned that the self-righting reflex always begins at the head. When a cat feels itself falling, it immediately brings its front paws close to its head. It then twists its upper spine so that its head is upright and parallel to the ground—this straightens the front half of the cat's body. Next the cat lowers its front legs. Finally it twists its lower spine to straighten the rear half of its body, lowers its hind legs, and lands on all four paws, arching its back to help absorb the shock of impact.

Unfortunately, cats' extraordinary balance and their ability to land on their feet have led some people to believe that cats are safe in high places and that falls don't hurt them. But veterinarians know that falls from open windows, balconies, or other high places are one of the most common causes of injury and death in pet cats.

Cats' internal systems, while basically similar to those of all mammals, have some distinctive features. The cat's normal internal temperature of 101.5 degrees Fahrenheit (38.6° C) is somewhat higher than a human's, which is why a cat warms a lap or a bed. Cats also tolerate and even enjoy higher temperatures than people can bear. They like to sleep in patches of sun or near fires, even going so far as to nap on radiators too hot for their owners to touch. However, cats do need to cool themselves when they become overheated—in very hot and humid weather, for example. Their skin does not have sweat glands, so they release water from the lungs and mouth by panting. The evaporation of this excess moisture into the air produces a cooling effect.

The cat is a carnivore, but its digestive system differs from those of some other carnivores. Dogs, for example, have the biochemical processes to obtain nutrients and energy from both

Scientists believe that cats use their tails to help them balance while they are in motion. Still, whether they were born without tails or lost them in accidents, tailless cats move and jump perfectly well.

The self-righting reflex is a series of moves that allows falling cats to land on their feet. It is probably one source of the saying that "cats have nine lives." But although a cat may survive a fall that would be fatal to another animal, many cats each year are injured or killed in falls.

plant and animal sources. This is why dogs (and bears) can eat both kinds of food and can survive reasonably well for extended periods without meat. Felines, however, must consume food from animal sources. They may eat plants and vegetable foods, but they cannot digest them or obtain necessary nutrients from them. Cats often chew and swallow grass, but they do not use the grass as food—it helps clean their teeth and helps wads of groomed fur pass through their systems. Some pet owners who are vegetarians try to feed their cats all-vegetable diets. Most experts agree that this is a mistake that seriously threatens cats' health. "You can't turn your cat into a bird," says one vet, "and you can't turn it into a vegetarian, either. Cats living in the wild must eat meat. Pet cats must eat food that contains animal protein."

A cat's most visible feature is its coat of fur. Fur is thickest on cats' bellies, thinnest on their backs. The coat is made up of three kinds of hairs. Down hairs are soft, short, and fine. Lying close to the cat's body, they form a warm layer called the undercoat. Awn hairs are longer and somewhat bristly. They form the middle coat. Longest and straightest are the guard hairs of the topcoat. Shinier than other hairs, guard hairs offer protection against damp. Wildcats have about 300 awn hairs and 20 guard hairs for every 1,000 down hairs, but in domestic cats these ratios are more variable, as are the color markings and hair lengths. Guard hairs reach 5 inches long in some Persians, and even cats that are basically shorthaired can have ruffs (longer or thicker hair around their necks), breeches (longer or thicker hair on the upper backs of their legs), or fluffy tails.

Vibrissae—better known as whiskers—are highly specialized hairs. Thicker than guard hairs, they are instruments of the cat's sense of touch. Cats usually have about two dozen whiskers on their upper lips, with a few others on their cheeks, eyebrows, and chins.

WHISKERS ARE LONG, STIFF HAIRS THAT PROBABLY SERVE SOME SPECIAL PURPOSE, BUT
SCIENTISTS ARE NOT CERTAIN WHAT THAT PURPOSE IS. SOME RESEARCHERS THINK
THAT WHISKERS HELP CATS SENSE OBJECTS OR OBSTACLES CLOSE TO THEM ON EITHER
SIDE WHEN VISIBILITY IS POOR.

Not all parts of the cat are fur-covered. The skin on the nose and paw pads is tougher than the rest of the cat's skin but also very sensitive. Patterns of tiny ridges in the skin of the nose are unique to each cat, like fingerprints.

Feline Senses

Cats' senses operate in ways well suited to a life of hunting in the wild. Their sight is adapted to seeing well at night or in low light. Like many nocturnal animals, cats have a layer of reflective tissue in each eye that increases their ability to gather light from the environment. This layer, called the tapetum lucidum, is what causes cats' eyes to glow an eerie green or yellow when light from headlights or flashlights shines on them at night. Cats also have binocular vision, which means that the fields of vision from their two eyes overlap. Eyes that work together allow the cat to judge size, depth, and distance—a valuable ability in a hunter that stalks and pounces on its prey. Cats are, however, at least partly color-blind. Scientists have not determined for certain which colors cats can perceive, but there is good evidence that they see only two colors. Red, orange, yellow, and green probably appear as one color, blue and violet as another. But there is no way to know exactly what those two colors look like to a cat.

A cat's hearing is far better than that of a human being or even a dog. In fact, some zoologists think that the only creatures with better hearing than cats are bats and some kinds of insects. Cats can hear sounds at very high frequencies, such as the high-pitched squeaks of moles and mice, which would be inaudible to other animals.

Smell and taste are closely interwoven in cats; some researchers group them together and call them the chemical senses. Smell is an important part of a cat's world. Although a cat's sense

CATS' EYES OFTEN SEEM TO SPARKLE OR GLOW BECAUSE THEY ARE LINED WITH
MEMBRANES THAT REFLECT LIGHT. AT NIGHT THEY GLEAM BRIGHTLY WHEN CAUGHT
IN A BEAM OF LIGHT.

of smell is far less keen than a dog's, it is about thirty times better
than a person's. Scent does not seem to play a great role in hunting, but it is vitally important in cat-to-cat communication. Each
cat's urine carries a unique odor that identifies the cat to other
cats. Cats also recognize familiar places and people by scent. In
addition, they seem to enjoy certain smells simply for their own
sake. Cats that have a strong liking for some foods over others

probably base their preference on smell rather than taste. In addition, some cats seem to like to be near particular perfumes or scented lotions, and about half of all cats respond strongly to the smell of the herb catnip, which both excites and relaxes them. Cats that like catnip often display a behavior called flehmen breathing, during which they curl back their upper lips and draw breath through their open mouths. This allows air carrying scent molecules to pass over both the tongue and a special scent gland called the vomeronasal organ, located in the roof of the cat's mouth. Flehmen breathing seems to combine the features of smell and taste, and cats often use it to test new odors. The sense of pure taste is less highly developed in cats than smell is, although even very young kittens recognize the differences between plain and slightly salty water.

The sense of touch is highly developed in cats. They use their noses, paws, and whiskers to investigate their environments. The skin of a cat's nose is very sensitive to temperature, and a cat that seems to be smelling liquid or food may really be placing its nose near enough to tell whether the substance is too hot to eat or drink. Cats use their flexible paws to touch and move objects and to pat their kittens, each other, and their owners. The guard hairs in the cat's coat are also linked to touch receptors in the skin and nervous system, which is why a cat feels even the gentlest touch or brush of wind against its body. The stiff whiskers appear to be tools for touching, although experts are not certain exactly how they work. They may help cats sense objects on either side of them in darkness.

Health Problems

Cats and people suffer from many of the same health problems, including cancer, kidney disease, arthritis, and diabetes. Cats can also fall victim to diseases or conditions that they can pass to humans, as well as some health problems that are specifically feline.

Rabies, an infectious disease usually spread by saliva through biting, is present throughout the animal world and is one of the most serious illnesses cats can catch. Sadly, once an animal (or a person) has developed full-blown rabies, there is no treatment, and the victim is almost certain to die. People stand a good chance of surviving, however, if they receive medical treatment immediately after being bitten by an infected animal. The best protection for cats that are around other animals is a preventive vaccination that reduces their chances of getting rabies.

Cats can also be vaccinated for protection against other infectious diseases caused by viruses. These include feline herpes virus (FHV), feline calicivirus (FCV), and feline rhinotracheitis virus. These cause symptoms often grouped together as "cat flu": sneezing, fever, runny eyes and noses. Most cats recover, but some cases are more serious and can lead to death. Another viral infection, feline leukemia (FeLV), often has serious consequences. It can cause cancer of the white blood cells and cancerous tumors throughout the body. Regular vaccination by a veterinarian can protect cats against these conditions, but there is no vaccine for feline immunodeficiency virus (FIV), the feline version of HIV, the virus that causes AIDS in humans. It weakens the cat's immune system, which can permit disease to take hold, but FIV cannot be passed to humans.

The same is not true of toxoplasmosis, a parasitic organism that can infect both cats and humans. Toxoplasmosis, which generally spreads through contact with feces that contain eggs of the parasite, can cause birth defects in unborn children. For this reason, pregnant women should not change a kitty litter box or handle cat feces. Cats can suffer from other parasites as well,

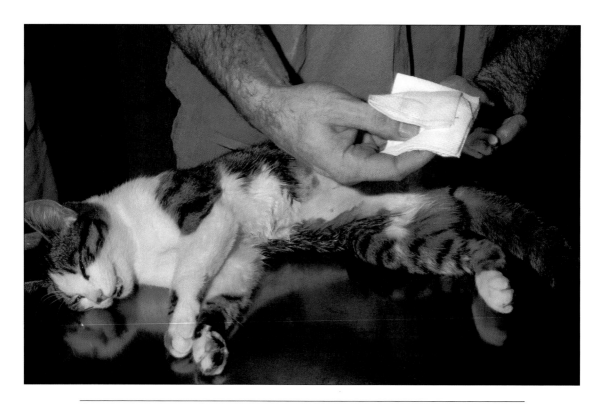

A VETERINARIAN REMOVES DISINFECTANT PADS AFTER PERFORMING A SPAYING, A SIMPLE OPERATION THAT PREVENTS A FEMALE CAT FROM HAVING KITTENS. (A SIMILAR OPERATION FOR MALE CATS IS CALLED NEUTERING.)

including fleas, roundworms, and tapeworms. Veterinarians can treat these infestations or give advice on commercial remedies.

The problems that most often bring cats to veterinary waiting rooms are injuries (usually caused by being struck by cars or falling); infected cuts, wounds, or bites (from fighting or stepping on sharp objects); and poisoning (from exposure to toxic materials such as petroleum, antifreeze, or disinfectant, and more rarely as a result of deliberate baiting with poisoned food). Dental disease, usually signaled by swollen or infected gums, is very common. Gum problems and broken teeth are not only painful but also can interfere with a cat's ability to eat. Veterinarians advise cat owners to clean cats' teeth regularly and can also perform such cleanings at their offices.

A cat's world can be dangerous. Although many cats survive to respectable ages without medical aid or veterinary care, life is certainly more comfortable for cats that receive it.

4

The Life Cycle

Kittens may be the most immediately lovable of all creatures. Big-eyed, adorably fluffy, curious, and playful, they are so cute that they appear on uncountable millions of greeting cards, calendars, and knickknacks. Only a hardened ailurophobe, as those unfortunate folk who fear or dislike cats are called, could fail to smile at the sight of kittens. Yet kittens, appealing as they are, represent a problem that should concern every cat owner. Many thousands of unwanted kittens are born each year. All too often, people whose pets have produced kittens must scramble to find homes for them, and when they fail, some simply abandon the unwanted young. As a result, animal shelters overflow with homeless kittens and cats, many of which must be put to sleep if they are not adopted. Having kittens in a home is a wonderful thing—as long as those kittens are guaranteed permanent homes. But cat owners who do not wish to be responsible for kittens' futures, and those who allow their cats to roam freely

PEOPLE HAVE CARRIED CATS TO ALL PARTS OF THE WORLD. THESE KITTENS GREET THE SUN ON A DOORSTEP IN ECUADOR, SOUTH AMERICA. THEY ARE VERY YOUNG AND HAVE PROBABLY NOT BEEN OUT OF THE NEST FOR LONG.

outside the house should consider a safe, simple veterinary surgery that prevents cats from reproducing. Called neutering in male cats and spaying in females, this surgery removes part of a cat's reproductive system. Veterinarians encourage neutering and spaying unless kittens are definitely wanted. Some cat owners believe that spayed and neutered cats are more satisfactory

A WORKER AT AN ANIMAL SHELTER IN NEWMARKET, ONTARIO, CANADA, WASHES A KITTEN—ONE OF THE HUNDREDS OF THOUSANDS OF HOMELESS OR ABANDONED KITTENS THAT END UP IN SHELTERS EVERY YEAR. IF THIS YOUNG FELINE IS LUCKY, IT WILL BE ADOPTED INTO A HUMAN FAMILY.

as house pets because feline courtship and mating behavior can be noisy, messy, and disruptive—at least from the human point of view. From a cat's point of view, however, it is what their species must do to survive.

Courtship and Mating

The cat's life cycle begins with the pairing of a female and a male cat, called the queen and the tom. An unneutered tom can mate at any time and will usually try to do so at any opportunity. Queens, however, mate only when they are in estrus, a state of readiness that usually occurs twice each year, once in late winter or early spring and again in late spring or early summer. Cats kept indoors may enter estrus more frequently and at other times of the year.

Estrus, sometimes called the queen's heat or season, generally lasts up to ten days, or until she is mated. At the start of estrus, the queen becomes restless and may pace, roll, or rub against people and furniture more than usual. Soon she begins calling, using a distinctive rising and falling yowl. This signal brings any nearby toms right to the queen. The queen also urinates more frequently and deposits a special scent from a gland in her reproductive system. All these signals are sure to attract toms. A queen in estrus that is kept indoors and not allowed to mate may become highly restless, scratching furniture, yowling incessantly, and trying to get out of the house. Meanwhile, toms may gather outside to serenade her with their own loud cries, or caterwauls.

A queen will mate with more than one tom during estrus, and male cats compete for the privilege of mating with her. Many confrontations between toms go no further than staring, hissing, and posing in a threatening manner, although all-out fights do take place as well. Sometimes, while two aggressive

CAT COURTSHIP IS A NOISY BUSINESS. FEMALES, CALLED QUEENS, YOWL LOUDLY AND OFTEN WHEN THEY ARE READY TO MATE. MALES, OR TOMS, MAY ANSWER WITH THEIR OWN CATERWAULS. TOGETHER THEY CAN WAKE ENTIRE NEIGHBORHOODS.

toms are fighting over a queen, a third, less combative male slips by them and mates with her.

Mating begins with a courtship period during which the male approaches the female slowly and carefully, circling her and sniffing her until he is certain that she is willing to accept him. This courtship can last for several hours or only minutes. The female signals her readiness to mate by crouching with her hindquarters raised and her tail held to one side, but even then the male must be cautious. Although she wants to mate, the queen may hiss, snarl, or even fight, if the male approaches too quickly. Finally he takes the loose skin at the back of her neck in his mouth. If she does not protest, he straddles her, and they mate. Mating does not take long, and as soon as it is complete the male jumps away, for the female usually growls, hisses, and swats at him. Within a few moments, though, she may be ready to receive him again. Queens can mate ten or even twenty times a day when first coming into estrus, and if they have the opportunity to mate with different toms, they may bear litters in which the kittens have different fathers.

Kittenhood

A queen that becomes pregnant carries her young for sixty-three to sixty-five days before giving birth. About halfway through this period her pregnancy becomes obvious, although a veterinarian can detect it much earlier by examining her gently.

A pregnant cat may eat and sleep more than usual. Two or three weeks before she is due to give birth, she begins looking for a nest site—a safe, dry, warm place in which her kittens will be born and spend their early days. Domestic cats find nest sites in closets or drawers, under beds, in boxes, or in special cat beds or houses provided by their owners, and they often carry favorite toys to these spots. A pregnant stray may seek out a nest site under a porch or in a barn or abandoned building.

Birthing a litter may take some time, as an hour or two can pass between kittens. The average litter size is four or five

kittens, but smaller and larger litters are not uncommon. A typical newborn kitten weights almost 4 ounces, although kittens of some slender breeds may weigh as little as 2 ounces. Each kitten is born in a sac of fluid, and the mother promptly licks it dry. Her licking also stimulates the kitten to begin breathing. The queen then nips off the kitten's umbilical cord and eats it. The kitten crawls to the mother's belly, where it nestles against her body and begins to suckle milk from one of her six or eight nipples. The kitten will return to that same nipple for every feeding until its mother weans it, or stops feeding it from her body. The mother stays very close to her kittens for the first few days of their lives, curling her body around them to keep them warm. Most mother cats purr while nursing their young, and some even purr while giving birth. The vibration of the purr may comfort the newborn kittens or help them to locate her. She licks them often so they know her smell and she knows theirs. She also must lick their genitals to urge them to begin eliminating waste.

Newborn kittens are helpless. Without care, they die. Kittens are born with their eyes closed and may not open them for up to ten days. (All cats' eyes are blue at first, changing to their adult color when the cat is between six and twenty weeks old.) For the first three weeks or so of their lives, kittens cannot walk well. They move by scooting themselves about and scrabbling with their paws; they cry and squeak if they become separated from their mother.

Newborn kittens spend most of their time sleeping, curled up together for warmth and security.

Young kittens nurse constantly, as much as eight hours a day. Kittens often knead or paddle with their paws on their mother's belly while they nurse. (This behavior, thought to increase the flow of milk to the nipple, can continue into adult life. Grown cats often make the same kneading motions on bathmats, blankets, cushions, or their owners' laps.) A mother cat's milk is about 10 percent protein and 6 percent fat, with more of both nutrients than human milk. Kittens grow quickly, doubling their weight during their first week. During their second week, their mother begins to leave the nest more often, for up to an hour at a time, but she still spends most of her time tending to her young.

By about four weeks, the kittens have begun to groom themselves and one another, to play by batting at objects and chasing tails, and to venture out of their nest. At this time kittens can be trained to use a litter box, a flat tray or shallow box containing sand or commercially prepared litter, a material that the cats can use to cover their urine and feces. Cats are naturally very clean and prefer to bury their waste. Nearly all house cats will readily use a litter box, if they can get to it easily and if it is kept clean, with frequent changes of litter. Kittens generally follow their mother to the box, but their owners can carry them there if they seem slow to learn.

When kittens are between four and eight weeks old, the mother cat may move them to a different nest. Cats living in the wild almost always change nests, carrying their young gently by gripping the loose skin behind the head in their teeth. Such moves are probably meant to protect kittens from predators drawn to the odors of long-used nests.

Many stories have been told about female cats' strong motherly instincts and fierce protection of their young. The maternal instinct is so strong in some cats that they will adopt

CATS THAT USE LITTER BOXES WILL PROBABLY TRAIN THEIR KITTENS TO USE THEM ALSO. LITTER BOXES MAKE IT POSSIBLE FOR CATS TO LEAD INDOOR LIVES.

A MOTHER CAT MOVES HER YOUNG FROM ONE NEST TO ANOTHER WHEN A KITTEN IS A FEW WEEKS OLD. NOTICE THE COLLAR—MANY CAT OWNERS "BELL" THEIR CATS TO GIVE WILD BIRDS SOME WARNING THAT A PREDATOR IS NEAR.

other cats' orphaned kittens, or even, in a few cases, orphaned rabbits or squirrels. Cats have also been known to go to heroic lengths to save their kittens from burning buildings, floods, and other dangers. Despite their protectiveness, domestic cats are usually willing to allow trusted and familiar humans to handle their kittens, although they may become anxious if the kittens are kept from them for long. If the young cats are expected to be domestic pets, it is a good idea to handle, groom, and stroke them gently. Research has shown that kittens that receive such treatment are usually friendlier, less timid, and more adaptable to new circumstances than cats that receive little stimulation or human contact.

Kittens that are old enough to move around outside the nest can get a wealth of excellent stimulation through play—with their siblings, toys, and their human family members. Cat owners can buy a wide variety of toys for kittens, but kittens have just as much fun with paper bags, balls of crumpled paper, and lengths of string or yarn dangled just out of reach or dragged along the floor.

KITTENS' FAVORITE TOYS MAY BE THEIR LITTERMATES. FELINE SIBLINGS PLAY GAMES OF POUNCING, WRESTLING, AND TUMBLING THAT HELP THEM DEVELOP PHYSICALLY, MENTALLY, AND SOCIALLY.

Play is more than just fun—it is a vital part of a young cat's growth. Games of running, chasing, and jumping help kittens develop physical strength, coordination, and balance. In addition, physical activity spurs mental development. Active kittens develop more nerve pathways in their brains than inactive ones. Finally, play is a way for kittens to learn important survival skills. Cats that catch and eat prey teach their young how to stalk, capture, and kill small animals, often bringing them live mice for practice. Even cats that eat only food provided by human owners teach their young the same skills, perhaps substituting a stuffed toy or catnip mouse for the real thing. Playful interaction—usually with siblings, but also with other cats and even dogs in households with different kinds of pets—also teaches a young cat how to get along with others. Kitten siblings engage in play-fighting, mock battles that allow them to practice aggressive moves such as biting and clawing without actually hurting one another. Feline mothers and young or siblings that remain together in a human household may remain playful and affectionate for years. Cats that go their separate ways, however, may not be especially friendly if they meet later.

Adulthood

Cats living under natural circumstances do eventually part. Mothers begin feeding their young bits of solid food at three or four weeks of age, or as early as two weeks in the wild. Gradually the young begin eating more and more solid food, although they still drink their mother's milk and will continue to do so until she refuses to let them suckle—usually by the eighth week of their lives. Kittens of domestic cats can usually be separated from their mothers by ten or twelve weeks of age if they have learned to eat fully independently.

Kittens of feral cats usually remain with their mothers until they are about twenty weeks old, at which point the queen may become pregnant again. If the young cats do not leave on their own, she may drive them away. Interestingly, students of cat behavior report that most cats become significantly less playful at about twenty weeks of age. Cat scientists think that twenty weeks may mark the end of a natural period of learning or adolescence. Older cats may still play, especially if they receive invitations to do so from their owners or from other cats, but play is no longer the all-consuming activity it once was.

The biggest change in a young adult cat's life is the arrival of sexual maturity, the point at which the cat becomes able to breed. Among domestic cats, most females reach sexual maturity between six and nine months old; males, between seven months and a year. Feral cats do not generally reach sexual maturity until they are fifteen to eighteen months old.

Queens can bear litters throughout much of their adult lives. After about eight years, though, the litters tend to become smaller, and after about eleven or twelve years, most queens will not become pregnant even if they mate. Males remain sexually productive later in life and may still father kittens at the age of fifteen years or even older.

Life span is one area in which domestic cats differ dramatically from cats that live in the wild. Research into the lives of feral cats suggests that they seldom live beyond ten years, and this seems to be the case for true wildcats as well. Wildcats and feral cats possess hunting and survival skills but are also subject to accidents, injuries, and being eaten by other carnivores.

The average life span of a domestic cat is about fourteen years, although many cats live much longer, especially if they have enjoyed a lifetime of good nutrition and veterinary care. Studies of cat behavior and body function suggest that a feline

These cats' owners let their pets enjoy a familiar yard or garden from time to time, but when the cats go outdoors they wear collars with identification tags. Another method of identification involves a microchip placed under the animal's skin by a veterinarian. If the cat becomes lost, a vet or animal shelter can scan the chip and notify the owner.

age of ten is about equal to a human age of sixty, which means that cats live a significant portion of their lives as elderly animals. Older cats have special needs. They may begin losing their sight or hearing, which causes them to react nervously to unexpected sounds and motions or to changes in their environment. Older cats are also less able to tolerate cold or hot temperatures and tend to sleep more and play less than younger adult cats.

Good care can prolong a cat's life and improve the quality of that life, but at some point even the healthiest cat simply wears out. Old age may bring kidney failure, diabetes, or some other lingering, painful condition. Many pet owners choose to have their sick pets euthanized, or painlessly killed by their veterinarians, rather than see them suffer. Although often in the cat's best interest, this decision can be difficult to make, and the death of a pet cat for any reason can be as sorrowful as the loss of any other beloved friend.

5 Feline Behavior

One of the reasons so many people like cats is that their behavior is fascinating. Even the most affectionate, playful, or "tame" cat has an independent side. Cat lovers say that the best illustration of a cat's nature is the way it approaches an out-stretched hand, seeming eager to be petted, and then halts an inch away from the fingertips. A cat keeps part of itself always just out of reach, and that is part of its charm. The behavior that ailurophiles (cat lovers) find so endearing and yet perplexing is a blend of the cat's natural wildcat heritage and the unnatural conditions of life with humans.

Social Life

The social life of the wildcat is simple: it doesn't have one. The wildcat shares its first few months with its mother and siblings and then spends the rest of its life alone. Yet domestic cats, which belong

A DOMESTIC CAT CAN LEARN TO GET ALONG WITH OTHER HOUSEHOLD ANIMALS, INCLUDING THOSE THAT WOULD BECOME ITS PREY IN THE WILD.

to the same species, form lasting and apparently affectionate relationships with people, other cats, and even other kinds of animals. One theory is that domestic cats behave throughout their lives in the same way that wildcats behave as kittens. Some animal scientists think that the domestic cat lives its whole life in a sort of extended kittenhood—humans who feed and care for it take the place of its mother, while other household pets or even neighborhood cats fill the role of siblings. According to this theory, even mature cats that raise their own young somehow remain kittens in relation to their owners.

A domestic cat's social life is shaped largely by whether it is an indoor cat, an outdoor cat, or a cat that moves back and forth between the house and the outside world. Cats raised entirely indoors adjust very well to an indoor life, whether spent in a small apartment with one owner or as part of a houseful of people and other pets. Indoor cats are less likely to be hit by cars, get into fights with other animals, or be exposed to disease. They are unlikely to be stolen or lost, and often they will not kill live prey. Outdoor cats, on the other hand, do kill prey, and they also encounter various dangers. Still, some cat owners believe that roaming outdoors is a more natural way of life for a cat than being cooped up in a house.

Whether a feral cat living in a suburban park, a farm cat living in a hay barn, or a pet that can go inside a house whenever it wants to, any cat outdoors must get along with other cats. Domestic cats do this the same way wildcats do—by establishing territories. A cat's territory may be as small as a windowsill or as large as a city block. It may even overlap the territories of other cats. Cats that are more dominant or aggressive than others in an area tend to have the largest territories or those considered most desirable, such as gardens with access to birds or mice instead of paved lots or rooftops. A cat's territory might be

LIKE MANY OLD SAYINGS, THE PHRASE "FIGHTING LIKE DOGS AND CATS" IS NOT ALWAYS TRUE. A DOG AND A CAT CAN LIVE IN HARMONY, ESPECIALLY IF THEY GROW UP TOGETHER OR IF ONE IS STILL VERY YOUNG WHEN THEY ARE INTRODUCED.

the yard of its owner's house, but it might also extend into a neighbor's yard or be limited to only a portion of its own yard.

Cats mark the borders of their territories with urine, feces, scratch marks on vertical surfaces such as tree trunks and fences, and scent from special glands in the face and near the anus. These markings are signs of territorial ownership, and cats refresh them often. By smelling another cat's scent marking, a cat can tell not only who made it but how long ago. Indoor cats also have territories, ranging in size from the entire house to a favorite cushion or chair. Although most indoor cats soon learn not to leave urine and feces around the house, they rub their scent glands on things (including their owners) to mark them as theirs. They also may have the urge to scratch. Some owners trim their cats' claws or have them removed by a veterinarian, although providing an appropriate place for the cat to scratch usually solves the problem. A cat that goes outdoors, even occasionally, should never be declawed. Its claws are a vital piece of protection, necessary for fighting off other animals or climbing trees to escape danger.

Most of the time, cats respect one another's territories. They would rather avoid one another than get into confrontations or fights. Conflict is usually settled by hissing and chasing rather than serious fighting. The worst trouble occurs when new cats enter an area or when toms gather to compete for mating rights. At other times, cats in adjoining or overlapping territories generally ignore one another.

The feline population of an area is likely to include cats that live in different ways. The wildcats of Europe, Asia, and Africa are entirely wild and almost never interact with other cats or people. Domestic or pet cats, in contrast, have homes and owners, even though they may spend a fair amount of time roaming freely. Between these two extremes are stray and feral cats.

Strays are cats that have become lost or have been abandoned. If they are young or have had no experience hunting prey, they may not be able to survive on their own. Some stray cats are reunited with their owners or taken in by new owners. Others end up in animal shelters. Some continue to live wild or semi-wild, joining the population of feral cats. These are cats that were once domestic animals but have adjusted to life on their own, or they are the offspring of such cats. Some feral cats live just like wildcats, surviving entirely on prey. Others scavenge in dumps and garbage bins or receive handouts from people. In some places people regularly put out food for feral cats living in the streets or in parks.

Some free-roaming feral cats do something that wildcats never do: they live together in groups or colonies that may remain stable for generations. These colonies often form around a food source such as a dump, a fishing dock, a farm, or a park where people leave food. One of the most unusual features of these colonies is that queens with kittens may share their nests and nurse one another's young. Animal scientists are studying feral cat colonies in an attempt to discover why these cats behave in a manner so different from that of their truly wild cousins. One theory is that feral cats—which were originally domesticated—learned to be social as members of human households. They then passed their social culture from one generation to the next in training their kittens, so that even cats that have never lived with people still give evidence of the way humans have reshaped the wildcat.

In addition to scent markings, cats use body language and voice to communicate with their young and with other animals or people around them. In early kittenhood cats begin to master a set of postures and movements that express anger, fear, pleasure, interest, and various ways of saying "Leave me alone."

Unlike wildcats, domestic and feral cats interact with one another frequently and often form communities. Each of these cats sunning itself on a rooftop in Provence, France, has a small territory somewhere that it regards as its own. The cats are also comfortable in a shared or group territory with little space between members.

Staring is a threat—two male cats, for example, may stare fixedly at each other until one backs down and moves away. Ears are very expressive. When cocked forward, they indicate attention or curiosity. Turned outward, they are a sign of displeasure, even anger. Ears laid flat indicate a cat that feels trapped or threatened and may react violently. A cat that arches its back, often

AN ARCHED BACK SHOWS FEAR, WHICH CAN EASILY TURN INTO AGGRESSION IF THE CAT FEELS CORNERED OR THREATENED.

with fur standing on end, is feeling both fearful and aggressive, although the reaction may pass quickly if the cat decides there is nothing to fear. A lashing tail is also a sign of fear, aggression, or both. On the other hand, a cat that wants to yield or submit to a more dominant animal may roll over to expose its belly. Some cats use the same move when they are feeling comfortable, relaxed, and secure with their owners.

Cats use their voices to communicate in certain circumstances. Females and males call to one another when females are in estrus. Kittens cry for their mothers, and mothers may respond with low chirping or murmuring sounds. Mother cats and kittens also purr to one another when the kittens are nursing, making a distinctive rumble that is as much vibration within the body as it is sound. Purring has mystified researchers for years, but the most recent studies show that it is caused by a regular and frequent tremor, or shaking, of nerves leading to the cat's diaphragm (a muscle used in breathing) and its vocal cords, which produce sound. Many researchers think that mother cats and kittens purr as a "contact" sound that reinforces their bond. Cats then go on to use the purr when mating, being groomed, or experiencing other social situations.

The sound most closely identified with the cat is usually spelled *m-e-o-w* (the ancient Egyptian word for "cat" translates from their language as *myw*). Cats vary the tone and volume of their meows to express greeting, curiosity, desire for food or attention, or loneliness. Hostility is more likely to be expressed with a low growl, a hiss, or a snarl. Fear, rage, or injury may cause a cat to produce a loud, high-pitched yowl. All in all, cats manage to communicate quite well without words, even to members of other species. Anyone who has ever seen a cat with ears flattened, fur bristling, and tail lashing and heard its spitting hiss or warning snarl has no doubt about its intended message.

A cat's typical day depends upon whether it is domestic or feral, indoor or outdoor, and a host of other factors. Some things, however, are much the same for all cats.

Wildcats are semi-nocturnal, which means that they are often active at night, dawn, or dusk but may also be active by day. Neither wildcats, feral cats, nor domestic cats follow a set schedule of waking and sleeping, although many cats are most active around dawn and dusk. Cats sleep at any time of the day. Many indoor cats adjust themselves to the schedules of their human companions and sleep through much of the night while their owners are asleep, but they also nap frequently during the day. A typical adult cat spends about 50 percent of its time asleep, but its twelve daily hours of shut-eye are broken up into many light "catnaps" and periods of deeper sleep separated by waking intervals. Kittens spend more time asleep, about 60 to 70 percent of the day, and older cats may sleep for 75 percent or more. The highly flexible cat can sleep in almost any position but usually stretches out flat or curls into a circle for deep sleep.

Cats that catch their own food spend a fair amount of their waking time hunting. Even cats that receive a full serving of food at home each day may hunt if they are allowed outdoors. Cats generally lie in wait for prey to appear and then creep up on it, and good hunters are skilled in choosing the right places to wait—near mouse holes or bird feeders, for example. Research shows that cats typically make ten attempts for every successful catch. In general they kill more mice, voles, and other small rodents than birds. Mother cats bring prey home to their young, first feeding them bites and later letting them finish killing the prey themselves. In the same way, a house cat that hunts may deposit injured or dead birds or mice on the doorstep or bring

Since ancient times people have realized that keeping a cat around is a good way to control mice. Even a well-fed pet cat would find this mouse hole fascinating—and would try to catch its inhabitant.

them into the house, sometimes even offering these trophies to their owners with the air of one graciously presenting a generous gift.

Grooming is another important activity that may take up as much as a third of a cat's waking time. Cats use their tongues, which are covered with tiny spikes called papillae, both to wash and to comb their coats. By twisting its flexible spine, a cat can lick almost all of its body. It uses its paws, moistened with saliva, to wash its head and ears. Cats also use their incisors, or front teeth, to nip burrs and other objects out of the fur on their bodies and between their toes. Cats that are housemates often groom each other, and many cats enjoy being combed or brushed by their owners.

Intelligence

How intelligent are cats? Dog lovers sometimes argue that cats are less intelligent than dogs because they do not do tricks. The cat lover's response is usually, "Well, of course. Cats are too smart to do tricks!" Yet cats can, in fact, be trained to perform a variety of elaborate tricks or to behave in certain ways. The best way to train them is to reward them with treats or attention for doing well. Punishing cats for doing poorly backfires, causing them to become hostile or lose interest entirely. Although cats can learn many things, they cannot be relied on to perform consistently—they do what people want them to do only when *they* want to do it. This is why cats do not guide the blind, sniff for drugs or bombs, or do any sort of regular work. (Many cats have, however, "earned their keep" by catching rats and mice. A British post office even paid a cat a small weekly salary for many years for its services as a mouser. The money was used to pay for cat food, veterinary care, and a cat bed.)

CATS GROOM THEMSELVES REGULARLY WITH TONGUE, TEETH, AND PAWS. THEY ARE
NOT VAIN ABOUT THEIR LOOKS, BUT ARE SIMPLY FOLLOWING INSTINCTS SHAPED BY
LIFE IN THE WILD. CLEAN, SMOOTH FUR IS BETTER AT KEEPING A CAT WARM AND DRY
THAN FUR THAT IS DIRTY, ROUGH, OR TANGLED.

Laboratory research has shown that cats have good memories and can learn problem-solving skills. One series of experiments involved what scientists call object-discrimination problems, in which cats were encouraged to choose one wooden object over another of a different shape and color. The cats received food treats for making the correct choices. At the beginning of the study, cats needed dozens of attempts with each new pair of objects before they consistently got the right answer 80 percent of the time. But after about sixty problems, cats could reach 80 percent accuracy in just ten tries. Another set of experiments seemed to suggest that kittens could learn how to operate a food-releasing machine by watching adult cats do it. No other animal besides primates (the family that includes monkeys, apes, and humans) has been known to acquire knowledge this way, which is called observational learning. However, other explanations may exist for the kittens' successes, and further research is needed before scientists can be sure that cats learn how to do things by watching what goes on around them. But cat owners who have discovered that their pets have unlatched cupboards and opened windows will not be surprised if researchers find that it is true.

6 Cats Today

There have always been people who admire and love cats. Felines can inspire almost ridiculous levels of affection, as in the legend of the Chinese emperor who cut off the jeweled sleeve of his priceless robe rather than disturb a kitten that had fallen asleep on it. Yet for many years, at least in the Western world of Europe and the United States, society as a whole seemed to view cats with some suspicion. Dogs were symbols of loyalty, faithfulness, and companionship. Cats were often portrayed as sly and untrustworthy, if not downright mean. Such images are common in art and popular culture, from the painting by fifteenth-century Italian artist Domenico Ghirlandaio that shows a cat as the companion of Judas, the betrayer of Jesus Christ, to *The Cat in the Hat*, who wreaked havoc on a modern suburban household.

To some extent, anti-cat attitudes linger. *The Character of Cats*, published in 2002, reported a survey that found that 17 percent of Americans dislike cats, but only 3 percent dislike

THE CAT IN THE HAT, CREATED IN 1957 BY CHILDREN'S-BOOK AUTHOR DR. SEUSS, IS ONE OF THE MOST FAMOUS FELINES IN THE WORLD. HE CAME TO PLAY ON A RAINY DAY—AND THE REST IS HISTORY.

ONCE CREATURES OF FORESTS AND FIELDS, CATS NOW OCCUPY EVERY NICHE IN THE MODERN WORLD. THIS STREET CAT IS AT HOME IN ONE OF THE WORLD'S BUSIEST URBAN AREAS, WALL STREET IN NEW YORK CITY.

dogs. Strangely, however, cats have outnumbered dogs as pets since the 1980s. In 2002 Americans owned about 75 million pet cats, compared to 60 million dogs. And likable or amusing cats are just as common in art, literature, and popular culture as mean or sly ones.

Some observers think that the rise in cat ownership is related to the conditions of modern life. Many people live in urban apartments—environments that some consider more suitable to cats than to dogs. Litter-trained cats require less attention than dogs, which must be taken outside several times a day, so cats are better pets for people with busy schedules. Whatever the reasons for its rise in popularity, the modern pet cat is at the center of a multibillion-dollar business. Manufacturers sell a wide range of cat products, from food and litter in all price ranges to toys, flea-control products, beds, and even caskets for funerals.

Cats are big business.

Yet cats are also a source of problems and controversies. One issue concerns feral cats, which number about 40 million in the United States and many times that worldwide. Feral populations can become breeding grounds for diseases that are passed on to domestic animals. They also produce enormous numbers of kittens. Some animal-care groups are experimenting with capturing feral cats, spaying or neutering them, and releasing them. They believe that this strategy will eventually cause feral cat colonies to die out, but results so far have not been promising. Feral colonies tend to remain stable because new cats join all the time. Others argue that feral cat colonies should be left alone, and that in time they will create new populations of animals much like wildcats.

Wildcats, however, are not native to the Americas, Australia, New Zealand, or many other islands. The growth of feral cat populations in such places has been disastrous for animals that

FERAL CATS MANAGE TO SCROUNGE A LIVING IN MANY UNPROMISING SETTINGS, OFTEN WITH THE HELP OF SYMPATHETIC PEOPLE WHO PUT FOOD OUT FOR THEM.

did not evolve to live in an environment that includes feline predators. Throughout history people have welcomed cats as destroyers of grain-eating rodents, but many are now concerned about excessive predation by feral cats—and by domestic cats that are allowed to roam and prey.

Most researchers agree that mice and other small mammals are the most common prey of cats, but they also kill enormous numbers of wild birds, and some cats prefer birds. Feline predation is very damaging to bird populations and is one of the chief reasons for concern about the rise in the number of feral cats.

Owners of domestic cats that go outside can limit their pets' damage by making sure that cats wear collars with bells and by keeping the animals indoors during birds' peak feeding hours, which are generally soon after sunrise and sunset.

Another controversy concerns cats and medical or scientific experimentation. While many projects that investigate cat behavior do not physically hurt the animals, thousand of cats are used each year in other, more painful research projects. New medicines and surgical procedures for people are tested on cats, and cats are frequent subjects of research into how the brain and nervous system work. Animal-rights groups frequently use heart-wrenching photographs of laboratory cats to arouse public feeling against animal testing in general. And some who can accept testing on rats or mice don't like the idea of cats being used in the same way, perhaps because it is easier to think of cats as companions that we invite into our lives.

For the same reason, many people object to the practice of eating cats, which is traditional in a few Asian countries. Even in places where certain kinds of cats have long been admired and kept as pets, strays and feral cats can still be regarded as food animals. Westerners may object to this practice, but in some parts of the world eating a cat seems no more unusual than eating a pig. The arrival of new Asian immigrants in Europe, Canada, and the United States, however, has led to a few accusations of cat murder.

The survival of many species around the world is threatened, but cats' future seems secure now that they have linked their lives with ours. The number of true wildcats remaining in Europe, Asia, and Africa is unknown, but experts estimate that it is in the millions. That number will surely shrink as wild habitat becomes rarer. The number of domestic cats, however, will probably continue to rise. Although many people have tried to

A PERFORMING CAT IS PART OF THE SUNSET SHOW ON THE PIER AT KEY WEST, FLORIDA. MOST CATS WILL NEVER DO TRICKS OR DELIGHT TOURIST AUDIENCES, BUT THEIR ORDINARY FELINE BEHAVIOR—THE RESULT OF THOUSANDS OF YEARS OF BLENDING WILD AND TAME TRAITS—WILL CONTINUE TO WARM THE HEARTS OF THOSE WHO LOVE THEM.

explain what makes cats so special, three writers perhaps offer the best insights to their appeal. French philosopher Hippolyte Taine wrote, "I've met many thinkers and many cats, but the wisdom of the cats is infinitely superior." Scottish novelist and poet Sir Walter Scott observed, "Cats are a mysterious kind of folk. There is more passing in their mind than we are aware of." And, most simply of all, from Great Britain's Christopher Morley: "What fun to be a cat!"

Glossary

adapt—to change or develop in ways that aid survival in the environment

ancestral—having to do with lines of descent

archaeologist—a scientist who studies the remains of earlier human settlements and cultures

breed—a variety of animal within a species that has distinctive physical features

carnivore—an animal that eats meat

chromosome—a structure within a cell on which genes are arranged

conservation—actions aimed at saving or preserving wildlife or its habitat

domestic—belonging to a species that has been domesticated or changed from a wild animal into one that humans raise, control, and use

evolve—to change over time

evolution—the process by which new species, or types of plants and animals, emerge from old ones

extinct—no longer existing; having died out

felid—a member of the family Felidae, which includes lions, tigers, jaguars, leopards, cheetahs, lynx, pumas, and many species of small cats

feline—a cat (noun); having to do with cats (adjective)

feral—referring to an animal that was once domesticated but now lives like a wild animal, or a wild-living animal descended from domesticated ancestors

genetic—having to do with genes, material made of DNA within the cells of living organisms. Genes carry information about inherited characteristics from parents to offspring

habitat—the type of environment in which an animal lives

mammal—an animal with a backbone that nourishes its young with milk from its mammary glands, and that has hair or fur. Cats and humans are mammals, as are thousands of other animals

nocturnal—active by night

predator—an animal that lives by predation, which means killing other creatures for food

prehistoric—before the invention of writing and the beginning of written history

zoologist—a scientist who specializes in the study of animals

Further Research

Books for Young People

Barrett, John. *Feral Cats*. Woodbridge, CT: Blackbirch Press, 1999.

Clutton-Brock, Juliet. *Cat*. New York: Dorling Kindersley, 2000.

Lumpkin, Susan. *Small Cats*. New York: Facts on File, 1993.

O'Neill, Amanda. *Cats*. New York: Kingfisher, 1998.

Parsons, Alexandra. *Amazing Cats*. New York: Knopf, 1990.

Zeaman, John. *Why the Cat Chose Us*. New York: Franklin Watts, 1998.

Videos

Cat Care. Atlanta: Northstar Entertainment, 1999.

Cats: Caressing the Tiger. Washington, D.C.: National Geographic, 1991.

Extraordinary Cats. New York: WNET-TV, 1999.

The Incredible World of Cats. New York: A & E Home Video, 1996.

Kittens to Cats. Beaverton, OR: Media West Home Video, 1987.

Web Sites

www.animaldiversity.ummz.umich.edu/accounts/felis/f._silvestris
    Maintained by the University of Michigan's Museum of Zoology, this
    site offers information on the scientific classification, biology, and
    behavior of the domestic cat.

www.lam.mus.ca.us/cats
    The Natural History Museum of Los Angeles County offers "Cats! Wild
    to Mild," with information on all kinds of felines, including domestic
    cats.

www.everything-you-ever-wanted-to-know-about-cats.com
> This ambitiously titled site has entries on cat care, the history of cats, and humor involving cats.

www.catsinternational.org
> An on-line file of articles on many aspects of cat care, biology, and behavior.

www.pbs.org/wnet/nature/excats
> Based on the PBS *Nature* show "Extraordinary Cats," this site has information on basic cat biology, stories about cats' abilities, and links to other Web pages.

www.nationalgeographic.com/features/97/cats
> *National Geographic*'s cat site is set up as an engineering project to design a perfect predator.

www.cfainc.org
> The Cat Fancier's Association site has links to the world's largest registry of pedigreed cats, descriptions of breed standards, and photos of prize-winning cats.

Bibliography

These books were especially useful to the author in researching this volume.

Altman, Roberta. *The Quintessential Cat*. New York: Macmillan, 1994.
An encyclopedia of cat history, legend, and lore from around the world, with entries on such subjects as celebrity cats, cats in cartoons and movies, and various breeds.

Bessant, Claire. *The Complete Guide to the Cat*. Hauppauge, NY: Barron's, 1999.
Overview of cat biology and behavior, with many color photographs.

Budiansky, Stephen. *The Character of Cats*. New York: Viking, 2002.
Readable, entertaining, and informative look at the latest scientific explanations of the origins, intelligence, and behavior of cats.

Fogle, Bruce. *Cats*. New York: Dorling Kindersley, 2000.
A lengthy and detailed survey.

Laroche, Robert, and Jean-Michel Labat. *The Secret Life of Cats*. Hauppauge, NY: Barron's, 1995.
Explores the role of cats in myth, legend, and art; beautifully illustrated with many color photographs.

Loxton, Howard. *99 Lives: Cats in History, Legend, and Literature*. San Francisco: Chronicle Books, 1998.

Morris, Desmond. *Cat Watching*. New York: Crown, 1986.
A famous zoologist examines feline behavior, communication, and personality.

Rogers, Katharine. *The Cat and the Human Imagination: Feline Images from Bast to Garfield*. Ann Arbor: University of Michigan Press, 1997.

Sayer, Angela, and Howard Loxton. *Encyclopedia of the Cat*. San Diego, CA: Thunder Bay Press, 1999.
An overview of all aspects of feline biology and behavior, with sections devoted to individual cat breeds and to cat ownership.

Tabor, Roger. *Cats: The Rise of the Cat*. London: BBC Books, 1991.
A survey of cat history based on a British television series of the same name.

Thomas, Elizabeth Marshall. *The Tribe of Tiger: Cats and Their Culture*. New York: Simon & Schuster, 1994.
A look at behavior in all species of felines, including domestic cats.

Wright, Michael, and Sally Walters, eds. *The Book of the Cat*. New York: Summit Books, 1980.
A detailed look at the evolutionary background, wild relatives, biology, behavior, and breeds of cats.

Index

Page numbers in **boldface** are illustrations and charts.

About the Author

REBECCA STEFOFF has written many books on scientific and historical subjects for children and young adults. Among her books on animal life are *Horses*, *Bears*, *Tigers*, and *Dogs* in Marshall Cavendish's AnimalWays series and the eighteen volumes of the Living Things series, also published by Benchmark Books. *Horses* was honored by the American Society for the Prevention of Cruelty to Animals for promoting a better understanding of the relationship between people and animals. Stefoff lives in Portland, Oregon.